Caring is Art

Gifts of appreciation
& encouragement

With quotes from caregivers

Words, Painting & Photography by
Leilani Norman

Caring is Art

Printed in the USA

Caring is Art, PO Box 1426, Bellingham WA 98227
(360) 922-7182

978-0-578-29906-8 (hardcover)
979-8-9869568-0-0 (paperback)

caringisart.com

Dedicated to the millions
of caregivers around the world,
with deep respect and admiration.

And to my mother,
Clara Kawahara Norman, CRNA.
She modeled caring for people with dignity,
kindness, and a sense of humor.

Caring is an art form that we practice daily,
no matter where we are on the caregiving journey.
The duration may be brief, or it may be for a lifetime.
This passage offers us many opportunities
to express our love through our presence, our labor,
our intentions, and our letting go.

Message from the Author

I created this book with the hope that it will validate your life of caring. Taking care of another person is both rewarding and challenging, filled with love and difficulty.

This is not meant to be an expert guide or a self-improvement manual, but a companion to you. I included resources that I have found useful and I hope that you will, too.

You will notice that there are several kinds of pages throughout; gentle self-care prompts, quotes from fellow caregivers, and resources. Because I am a visual artist, the fourth element I offer is beautiful images for you to enjoy.

Leilani Norman
Bellingham, Washington

"I cared for my father for eight months as my mom was experiencing caregiver burn out. It was at this time that my dad and I had the most real conversations we ever had."

— Leah

"My mother was a beautiful, fiercely independent woman. We did not always get along so well during my youth. Our strong wills were an equal match. I am happy to say that we really got close during her last 10 years. She came to respect and to admire my life and my accomplishments and was able to say this to me. It was very healing."

— Laura

"When talking to our Dad who had dementia, we could often see his frustration when asked a question he couldn't answer. We soon learned not to put him "on the spot" to answer. Instead, we gently guided the conversation by telling family stories, recollecting trips we took, great meals eaten, etc.

We were often surprised when it sparked something in his mind and he contributed perfectly to the conversation. The entire family became comfortable with this style of communication and visited him much more often."

— David & Mary

"I'm supporting my mother over a long distance, so
I can't visit with her in person as often as we both
would like. It is a challenge to deal with my feelings of
hopelessness, lack of control and guilt. Between visits,
I stay in touch with Mom through phone calls, cards,
letters and care packages."

— Sandra

"I lost my Dad to dementia. He was a World War II veteran, a trusted and respected member of the tiny community that I grew up in. He was a wise, kind, and supportive family man. I live by those values and morals today."

— Leslie

"It's okay to be as repetitious as your loved one. Come up with a sentence or mantra that helps you deal with difficult moments and repeat it when you need it. Mine was something like, 'I know this is hard for you.'"

— Denise

"The daily experience of caring for my mother ranged from fulfillment to heartbreak. When I learned to let go of who she used to be, I was able to attend to her evolving needs and to love her just as she was that day."

— Leilani

"Living on the other side of the world from my parents for most of my life, I knew that there was a strong likelihood that I would be far away when one of my parents died. When my father passed, I did not make it back in time to help care for him. I was so fortunate to be able to spend a month with my mother in her last year of life."

— Olga

You are not alone

Every five years, the National Alliance for Caregiving and AARP publishes the results of a family caregiving study. In 2020, researchers found that about one in five, or 53 million, Americans are unpaid caregivers, an increase of 9.5 million from 2015.

- The majority of family caregivers are between 61 and 75 years old.

- 61% are women.

- 24% are caring for more than one person.

- 23% of caregivers report that their own health has worsened while caregiving.

- 26% have trouble with coordinating care.

- 45% of caregivers have experienced at least one financial impact.

- 61% are providing care while employed.

Caregiving in the U.S. 2020
by National Alliance for Caregiving (NAC) and AARP

Lift Your Spirits

Tell the story that always makes you both laugh

Accepting Change

Can be difficult.

Kindness to ourselves is essential.

What can we gain from loss?

We begin by looking inside

Wisdom is a Superpower

 Citizen Brain: Age Without Ageism

Remind Yourself

You are loving, generous & kind.

 The Ups and Downs of Caregiving

Essentials for Caregivers

- Stay connected with family & friends

- Prioritize health for you and your care partner

- Find support for yourself

- Develop or strengthen your spiritual practice

- Keep legal and healthcare documents up to date

Courtesy of Leslie Jackson, RN
Education Coordinator, Dementia Support Northwest

Sharing is Caring

When we help others to help us

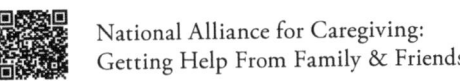

National Alliance for Caregiving:
Getting Help From Family & Friends

Move Like it Matters

Stretch periodically throughout the day.

 Two Minute Balance & Mobility Exercise

Fellowship

With other caregivers can help.

 Find a support group that works for you

Seek Respite

For yourself and your care partner.

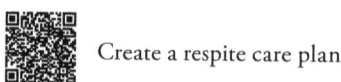 Create a respite care plan

Carrying a Burden

Awakens our empathy for all beings

Don't forget about yourself

Caregiver burnout can happen to anyone.

Signs may include:

Exhaustion that interferes with your daily life

Denial about your loved one's condition

Irritability and moodiness

Health problems

Sleeplessness

Anger or frustration with your care recipient

Anxiety and worry

Difficulty with concentration

Social withdrawal

 Family caregiver stress: signs and support

5-minute Break

Breathe in. Breathe out.

 Five Minute Bodyscan Relaxation

Isolation Can Happen

While we are busy providing care

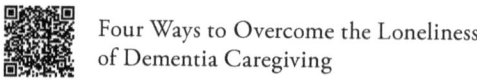

Four Ways to Overcome the Loneliness
of Dementia Caregiving

Consider the 5-Minute Vacation

Doodle.
Water the plants.
Confide in the dog.

Find a Moment for Yourself

Make a cup of tea.
Look out the window.

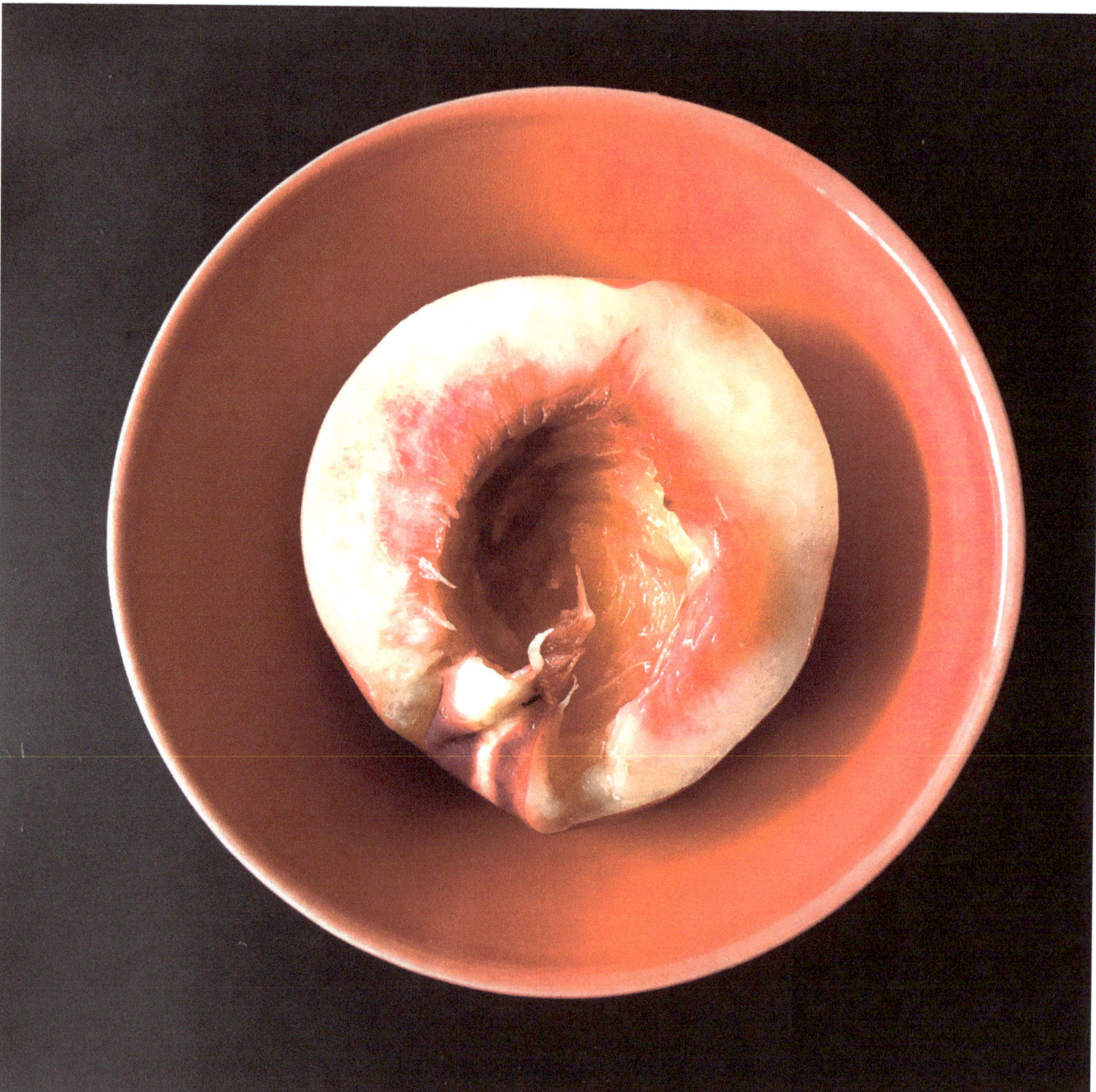

Be Impressed by Ordinary Beauty

Add something pretty & healthy to your diet

Resources in this book:

 Five Minute Relaxation
https://videos.aarp.org/detail/video/5128480877001/guided-breathing:-five-minute-relaxation---aarp?auto-Start=true&q=meditations

 Find a Support Group That Works for You
https://www.aarp.org/caregiving/life-balance/info-2021/support-groups.html

 Age Without Ageism
https://youtu.be/_7cIgjwZtPo

 The Ups and Downs of Caregiving
https://www.uhc.com/content/dam/uhcdotcom/en/IndividualAndFamilies/PDF/UA_SPRJ55113-the-ups-and-downs-of-caregiving.pdf

 Create a respite care plan
https://www.aarp.org/caregiving/life-balance/info-2017/respite-care-plan.html

 Four Ways to Overcome the Loneliness of Dementia Caregiving
https://dailycaring.com/4-ways-to-overcome-caregiver-loneliness-in-dementia-care/

 Two Minute Balance & Mobility Exercise
https://www.youtube.com/watch?v=wLef2W5PhQc

 Family Caregiver Stress: Signs & Support
https://www.mayoclinic.org/healthy-lifestyle/stress-management/in-depth/caregiver-stress/art-20044784

 Caregiving in the U.S. 2020
National Alliance for Caregiving (NAC) and AARP
https://www.caregiving.org/caregiving-in-the-us-2020/

 AARP Family Caregiving Resources
AARP.org

Area Agencies on Aging
https://www.usaging.org/

 Dementia Action Collaborative of Washington State
Dementia Road Map - A Guide for Family and Care Partners.pdf

 Family Caregiver Alliance
caregiver.org

 Living wills and advance directives for medical decisions
https://www.mayoclinic.org/healthy-lifestyle/consumer-health/in-depth/living-wills/art-20046303

 Understanding Advanced Medical Interventions
https://cedar.wwu.edu/pci/lectures_events/advance_care_planning/8/

 Understanding Palliative & Hospice Care
https://www.nia.nih.gov/health/what-are-palliative-care-and-hospice-care

Paintings by the author

Fleur, 2022, gouache and pen on paper, 16 x 16 in.
Blues, 2022, gouache and pen on paper, 16 x 16 in.
Blue Foothills, 2021, acrylic and pencil on canvas, 40 x 30 in.
Abundance, 2020, acrylic on canvas, 23 x 23 in.
Nine Eighteen, 2021, acrylic on wood panel, 40 x 30 in.
End of an Era, 2022, acrylic and pencil on canvas, 50 x 40 in.
Anthurium, 2019, gouache and pen on paper, 16 x 12 x 16 in.
Green Life, 2019, acrylic on canvas, 18 x 24 in.
Seeking the Path, 2021, acrylic on canvas, 24 x 36 in.
Verdure, 2020, acrylic on canvas, 48 x 36 in.
Inner Space/Dysmorphia, 2019, acrylic on canvas, 36 x 24 in.
*Stormy, 2021, a*crylic and pencil on canvas, 40 x 30 in.
Wildfire Sunset, 2022, gouache and pen on paper, 16 x 16 in.

For more information, visit leilaninorman.com

Photographs by the author

Green Lake, 2013
Picture Lake, Mt. Rainier Washington, 2018
LA Twilight, 2019
Fallen Leaf, 2021
Threshold, 2021
Coming or Going, Edmonds Washington, 2018
After the Storm, Long Beach Washington, 2017
Saltspring Boat House, 2019
Ueno Lily Pond, 2016
Claude's Window, 2017
White Peach, Red Bowl, 2021
Clematis, 2018
Floribundance, 2020

Photo Credits

Untitled, 2021, by Mina Young
Untitled, 2021, by Mina Young
I Heart the River, by Sandra Proctor

Notes

About the author:

Leilani Norman completed a twenty-year arc of support to her parents when her mother died in late 2021. She holds a certificate in Gerontology from the University of Washington and a BA in Psychology. Leilani is a visual artist, entrepreneur, award-winning designer, and parent.

This book was created to benefit organizations that provide support to caregivers of persons with chronic conditions.

Please support the caregivers in your life and in your community.

 caringisart.com

www.ingramcontent.com/pod-product-compliance
Lightning Source LLC
Chambersburg PA
CBHW041521120626
46551CB00018B/2518